Fall Prevention Training Guide
A Lesson Plan for Employers

A Guide for Employers to Give
Fall Prevention Training to Workers

OSHA® Occupational Safety
and Health Administration
U.S. Department of Labor

Safety Pays. Falls Cost.
www.osha.gov/stopfalls

OSHA 3666-08 2013

Table of Contents

Introduction

Falls cause more deaths in construction than any other hazard. In 2011, falls accounted for over a third of the 721 total construction deaths. Workers performing tasks 6 feet or more above lower levels are at risk of fatal falls or serious injuries.

This training guide will help you plan how to prevent injuries and fatalities from falls among your crew, and provide training to your workers. It includes the following tools:

- Instructions for using the Toolbox Talks to train workers in fall prevention *(pages 2–3)*.
- A series of Toolbox Talks about various fall prevention topics *(pages 5–12)*.

Additional resources:

- A Fact Sheet, in English and Spanish, with some key information about preventing falls *(page 15)*.
- A Wallet Card, in English and Spanish, which provides the web address for OSHA's Fall Prevention Campaign website and OSHA's contact information *(page 16)*.
- Easy-to-read OSHA posters, in English and Spanish, for the worksite and the community that you can copy and distribute to workers *(page 17)*.
- A bilingual booklet on ladder safety, *Falling Off Ladders Can Kill: Use Them Safely*, which can be read on any mobile device *(page 18)*.

The training is designed to be:

- **Short** — Each Toolbox Talk should last approximately 5-10 minutes. Although some talks contain more material than others, Toolbox Talks can be given at meetings before the work shift or during breaks.
- **Participatory** — Workers attending the talk should be able to ask questions and discuss the topic. This increases the likelihood they will remember the information.
- **Easy to follow**.

Why is it important to prevent falls?

- Preventing falls can mean the difference between life and death. Hundreds of workers die from falls each year. You can prevent such deaths by *planning* to get the job done safely, *providing* the right fall protection equipment, and *training* all workers to use the equipment safely.
- Many construction workers perform tasks at a height that requires protection from fall hazards.
- Having a serious injury or death occur at work affects everyone at a worksite.
- A fall can occur in a split second without any time for the worker to react.

Carrying out the training

Short and direct Toolbox Talks can be a very efficient way to reach workers with health and safety information. Like all training, delivering the information effectively takes preparation and a desire to involve the other workers in health and safety at the workplace. Employers may train workers to lead the training or have supervisors provide the training. Studies have shown peer-to-peer training is effective, participatory and well-retained.

In this guide, you will find advice for trainers that will encourage discussion and enable workers to actively participate in keeping the job site safe.

Follow these three steps to prepare and present a Toolbox Talk:

1. Read and become familiar with the next section, "How to use Toolbox Talks."
2. Give one of the Toolbox Talks.
3. Get feedback from the other workers. Did they understand the material? Was it well presented? How could the training be more relevant to their work?

How to use Toolbox Talks

The training guide is written so that you can easily follow it. The training is divided into three Toolbox Talks, each addressing a fall prevention topic. These include:

- **First Talk:** Ladder Safety
- **Second Talk:** Scaffolding Safety
- **Third Talk:** Roofing Work Safety

To provide this training, you will be leading a discussion in which you give an example of a fatality related to the topic, discuss how it could have been prevented, ask questions, and encourage participation.

How Toolbox Talks are formatted

- Each Toolbox Talk begins with an example of the types of incidents that are possible if workers do not follow the fall prevention guidelines outlined in the training.
- Following the job site example, the Toolbox Talk lists guidelines for preventing falls related to the topic (e.g., ladders).
- Finally, each training sheet includes blank lines for workers to include ways that the topic is applicable to their job site.

Preparing to teach the training sessions

1. Spend about 15 minutes to become familiar with the Toolbox Talk.
2. Print a copy of a relevant Toolbox Talk and think about how the topic relates to your specific worksite.
3. Look through the educational materials and resources listed at the end of the training guide, along with other materials on OSHA's web site, to find materials to supplement the Toolbox Talk.

Advice for trainers

Safety meetings work best if the whole crew actively participates. This makes it more interesting and more likely that people will remember the information you've given them. Here are some ways to encourage everyone to get involved:

- Ask questions instead of simply giving them the information. After you ask a question, wait a short time to let people think. Then, call on volunteers to answer.
- Ask about personal experience. This can help the group see how the topic is relevant to them. You could ask: Has anyone here fallen off a ladder? What happened?
- Make sure everyone has a chance to talk. If a crew member is talking too much, invite someone else to speak.
- Never make fun of anyone or put anyone down, especially for asking questions.

- Don't fake it. If you don't know the answer to a question, don't guess. Write the question down and promise to get back to them.
- Stick to the topic. If the crew's questions and comments move too far from the topic, tell them that their concerns can be addressed later, either privately or in a future safety meeting.

ToolboxTalks

Job site example

Ryan was applying sheetrock mud to a wall and was standing on the top rung of a 12-foot ladder. He lost his balance, fell to the concrete floor, and landed on his head. He suffered a major head injury.

Ladders are involved in many accidents, some of which are fatal. Your life literally can depend on knowing how to inspect, use and care for this tool. Let's spend a few minutes talking about ladders.

Inspecting ladders

Before using any ladder, inspect it. Look for the following faults:

- Loose or missing rungs or cleats;
- Loose nails, bolts, screws;
- Wood splinters or damaged edges;
- Cracked broken, split, dented, or badly worn rungs, cleats, or side rails; and
- Corrosion of metal ladders or metal parts.

If you find a ladder in poor condition, tag the ladder and take it out of service. If repairs are not feasible, the defective ladder should be removed from the job site.

Using ladders

Choose the right type and size ladder. Except where stairways, ramps, or runways are provided, use a ladder to go from one level to another. Keep these points in mind:

1. Be sure straight ladders are long enough so that the side rails extend above the top support point, by at least 36 inches.
2. Don't set up ladders in areas such as doorways or walkways where others may run into them, unless they are protected by barriers. Keep the area around the top and base of the ladder clear. Don't run hoses, extension cords, or ropes on a ladder and create an obstruction.
3. Don't try to increase the height of a ladder by standing it on boxes, barrels or other materials. Don't try to splice two ladders together.
4. Do not apply personal or job stickers/decals.
5. Set the ladder on solid footing against a solid support. Don't try to use a stepladder as a straight ladder.
6. Place the base of straight ladders out away from the wall or edge of the upper level about 1 foot for every 4 feet of vertical height. Don't use ladders as a platform, runway or scaffold.

7. Tie in, block or otherwise secure the top of straight ladders to prevent them from shifting.

8. To avoid slipping on a ladder, check your shoes for oil, grease or mud and wipe it off before climbing.

9. Always face the ladder and hold on with both hands when climbing up or down. Don't try to carry tools or materials with you.

10. Don't lean out to the side when you're on a ladder. If something is out of reach, get down and move the ladder over.

11. Most ladders are designed to hold only one person at a time. Use by two workers may cause the ladder to fail or throw the ladder off balance.

Care of ladders

Take good care of ladders and they'll take care of you. Store them in well-ventilated areas, away from dampness.

REMEMBER!

These safety practices may save you from a ladder tipping hazard!

How are ladders used on this job site and how will you use them safely?

_____

_____

Are you using a hazardous chemical while working on a ladder (such as paint primer or thinner) or performing roofing work (such as asphalt/roofing coating)?

If so,

Are Safety Data Sheets (SDSs), formerly referred to as Material Safety Data Sheets (MSDSs), provided for your review?

_____

_____

_____

_____

Are SDSs readily accessible?

_____

_____

_____

_____

Are all chemical containers labeled?

_____

_____

For assistance, contact us. We can help. It's confidential.

OSHA® Occupational Safety and Health Administration

U.S. Department of Labor
www.osha.gov (800) 321-OSHA (6742)

Second Talk: Scaffolding Safety

Job site example

Willie, a construction worker, fell 20 feet from an unsecured scaffold. He had been helping to install metal frames on the outer wall of a residential building when the accident happened. The leaning scaffold was not tied off, and while Willie was working, the scaffold moved away from the building. He then fell to the ground, hitting his head on the second story, and died.

It's a terrible thing to realize that hardly a work day goes by without a construction worker falling off a scaffold to his death. These deaths can be prevented.

Designing scaffolding

To avoid the use of makeshift platforms, each job should be carefully planned to assure that scaffolding is used when required and that scaffolding conforms to the applicable regulations.

- All scaffolds must be fully planked and constructed to support the load they are designed to carry. Scaffold planks must be cleated or secured, or extend over the end supports by at least 6 inches, but not by more than 12 inches.
- Ties, guys, and braces for a scaffold must be installed according to the scaffold manufacturer's recommendations. If the specifications are unknown then the standards at 29 CFR 1926.451(c)(1) must be followed.

- Barrels, boxes, kegs, horses, ladders, loose tile blocks, loose piles of bricks, A-frames or other unstable objects shall not be used as work platforms or to support scaffolds. Never use work platforms mounted on top of other work platforms.
- Guardrails, midrails and toeboards must be installed on all open sides of scaffolds, 10 feet or more in height.
- Falling object protection must be provided in areas where persons are required to work or pass under a scaffold.
- Overhead protection is required if employees working on scaffolds are exposed to overhead hazards.

Using scaffolding

1. Inspect scaffolds daily before you trust your life to them. Check guardrails, connectors, fastenings, footings, tie-ins, bracing and planking. Damaged scaffolds must be removed from service immediately.
2. Do not climb cross-bracing as a means of access.
3. Don't stockpile materials on scaffolds. Remove all tools and leftover materials at the end of the day.
4. Never overload scaffolds. Pile necessary materials over ledger and bearer points.
5. Keep platforms and area near the scaffold clear of debris, unneeded equipment or

material, and anything else that might cause you to slip or trip.

6. Use access ladders provided for each scaffold. Climbing off the end frames is prohibited.

7. In winter, clear platforms of all ice and snow before using. Sand wet planking for sure footing.

8. Never 'ride' a (mobile) rolling scaffold.

9. Only use a rolling scaffold on level surfaces, and lock caster breaks when not in motion. When moving, make certain the route is clear of holes and overhead obstructions. Secure all loose materials.

10. Use personal fall protection equipment tied off to an anchorage point from a lanyard, lifeline and/or deceleration device, when working from floats, needle beam scaffolds, or suspended scaffolds.

11. Protect ropes and safety lines from burning or welding.

Care of scaffolding

Help protect scaffolds, don't bang into them with equipment or materials. When hoisting material from the ground, control it with a tagline.

> **REMEMBER!**
>
> Give a scaffold the respect it deserves and it will serve as a convenient work platform.

How are scaffolds used on this job site and how will you use them safely?

_____

_____

_____

Are you using a hazardous chemical while working on a ladder (such as paint primer or thinner) or performing roofing work (such as asphalt/roofing coating)?

If so,

Are Safety Data Sheets (SDSs), formerly referred to as Material Safety Data Sheets (MSDSs), provided for your review?

_____

_____

_____

Are SDSs readily accessible?

_____

_____

Are all chemical containers labeled?

_____

_____

For assistance, contact us. We can help. It's confidential.

OSHA® Occupational Safety and Health Administration

U.S. Department of Labor
www.osha.gov (800) 321-OSHA (6742)

ToolboxTalks

Third Talk: Roofing Work Safety

Job site example

On June 6, 2011, John, a roofing professional, was working near an unguarded skylight installed on the roof of a one-story, commercial building, currently under construction. While installing roofing materials, he came in contact with an unprotected skylight and fell 18 feet to the floor below, fracturing only his right shoulder and rib. **John was extremely lucky!**

Many construction workers die from work activities performed near existing skylights, skylight openings, and other types of roof and/or roof opening hazards. As a result, roofing falls are the leading cause of death(s) on construction work sites. These fatal falls are attributed to: (1) failure to appropriately guard skylights and other existing roof openings, and (2) failure to provide effective fall protection training to workers in **hazard recognition** of serious fall hazards at the job site.

Fall prevention must be provided when working on steep roofs, open-sided floors, landings, or scaffold platforms, etc., whether the work activity is conducted by a general contractor, self-employed contractor, subcontractor or an individual worker.

What are fall hazards?

- Unprotected leading edge work
- Unprotected wall and floor openings

- Hoist areas
- Uncovered holes
- Roof and elevator openings
- Poor working surface integrity
- Unprotected ramps and runways
- Dangerous equipment
- Form work and reinforcing steel
- Excavations, wells and pits

What are the results of a fall hazard?

A fall hazard may result in death (fatality) or serious injuries such as permanent paralysis, blunt trauma to the head, broken bones, fractures, or other internal damage.

How to protect workers from fall hazards:

The **most effective** way to protect workers from falls is to eliminate the fall hazard. If this is not feasible, the employer is required to use at least one of the following:

- Personal Fall Arrest Systems **(PFASs)**, or fall restraints consisting of:

  a) **Anchorage** — A fixed and secured point of attachment for lifelines, lanyards, or deceleration devices capable of supporting 5,000 lbs. Sound anchorages include: structural members, but not standpipes, vents, other piping systems and electrical conduit.

  b) **Body Harness** — Straps which may be secured to the body in a manner which will distribute fall arrest forces over the thighs, pelvis, waist, chest and shoulders, with a means to attach to other components of a PFAS.

  c) **Connectors** — Devices used to couple/connect parts of the PFAS and positioning system devices together, e.g. a carabiner or an integral part of the system such as a dee-ring or buckle (sewn into a body harness) or a locking snap-hook.

  d) **Deceleration Device** — Any mechanism, such as a rope grab, rip-stitch lanyard, specially-woven lanyard, tearing or deforming lanyards, automatic self-retracting lifelines/lanyards, which serves to dissipate a substantial amount of energy during a fall arrest, or otherwise limit the energy imposed on an employee during fall arrest.

INSPECTIONS

Daily inspections are required prior to use of PFASs for wear damage, deterioration or other component defect and if observed, the PFAS must be immediately removed from service.

Other forms of fall protection systems include:

- Guardrail Systems – 1926.502(b),
- Safety Net Systems – 1926.502(c),
- Warning Line Systems – 1926.502(f),
- Controlled Access Zones – 1926.502(g),
- Safety Monitor Systems – 1926.502(h), and
- Hole Covers – 1926.502(i).

Fall prevention practices

Who has seen or heard of a worker who sat on a skylight for a break, a drink or a smoke, and then, the skylight breaks, and the worker falls onto the concrete floor below?

Yet we don't even need a skylight, or a floor opening to fall through a roof! We can over-load a roof with materials and equipment until the structure fails, or we may begin to work on an older roof without first inspecting the underside for signs of damage and/or decay.

What steps do we take to keep us working safely on roofs?

- Use PFASs or other fall protection systems, per the OSHA Fall Protection standard.

- Train workers in hazard recognition and the OSHA Fall Protection standard to properly identify and understand the severity of fall hazards and certify through written record.
- Guard or secure covers over holes with materials of sufficient strength, and write "Hole" over the cover upon observing the fall hazard.
- Provide and use safety monitor systems, warning line systems, or controlled access zones, in accord with the OSHA Fall Protection standard.

Personal fall arrest systems

When conducting roofing work, there are many ways to prevent fall hazards. If workers use a Personal Fall Arrest System (PFAS), the employer must provide a full body harness, lanyard and/or lifeline, per each worker, and an anchorage point independent of supporting any other platforms, but capable of supporting 5,000 lbs (22.2kN), per each attached worker. Make sure the PFAS fits the worker, and regularly inspect all fall protection equipment to ensure that it's still in good condition. If workers do not routinely use their PFAS, they may neglect routine daily inspection of their equipment — and when required to use their PFAS, a component part may fail!

Falls are the leading cause of death in the construction industry, and even experienced workers can be hurt and killed in falls. Regularly wear your PFAS, stay connected and tie-off to a proper anchorage point at the job site.

Safety monitor

Workers can use a safety monitor system in conjunction with a warning line system with a low slope roof (4:12 vertical to horizontal, or less), *under 50 feet or less in width*. The safety monitor must be a competent person and have no other duties that could interfere with their responsibility. They are required to work on the same level as the work being performed, and close enough to workers for direct monitoring (visual) and for verbal communication.

Let's discuss fall protection!

1. Have you received training in OSHA's Fall Protection standard?
2. Construction work at what level(s) require fall protection?
3. What conditions may lead to falls through a skylight, hole or over a ramp?
4. Is there a need to use fall protection at your job site?
5. What should the employer do to ensure that your job sites are free of unidentified fall hazards?
6. What OSHA standard applies?

Record questions below that you want to ask about this Toolbox Talk!

_____

_____

_____

Are you using a hazardous chemical while working on a ladder (such as paint primer or thinner) or performing roofing work (such as asphalt/roofing coating)?

If so,

Are Safety Data Sheets (SDSs), formerly referred to as Material Safety Data Sheets (MSDSs), provided for your review?

_____

_____

_____

_____

Are SDSs readily accessible?

_____

_____

_____

_____

_____

_____

_____

_____

For assistance, contact us. We can help. It's confidential.

U.S. Department of Labor
www.osha.gov (800) 321-OSHA (6742)

OSHA Educational Materials and Resources

The following OSHA Fall Prevention publications are provided in this *Fall Prevention Guide.*

- Fall Prevention Fact Sheet, OSHA 3533 – English
- Una hoja informativa—Prevención contra caídas, OSHA 3534 – Español
- Fall Prevention Wallet Card, OSHA 3557 – English
- Tarjeta sobre la prevención contra caídas, OSHA 3564 – Español
- Cartão de prevenção contra quedas, OSHA 3664 – Portuguese
- Fall Prevention Poster, OSHA 3531 – English
- Prevención de caídas—Cartel, OSHA 3532 – Español
- Falling Off Ladders Can Kill: Use Them Safely Booklet/Las caídas desde escaleras pueden ser mortales: Úselas de forma segura, OSHA 3625 – English/Español

Other OSHA publications:

Many OSHA publications are available in both English and Spanish, as well as Portuguese, Russian and other languages. To order multiple copies of these resources, call OSHA's Office of Communications at (202) 693-1999 or visit OSHA's Publications page at www.osha.gov/publications.

Adobe Reader is required to view PDF files.

Prevention Videos (v-Tools)

Videos are an effective educational tool. We have several workplace training videos based on true stories that are available online at www.osha.gov/stopfalls. The videos examine how falls lead to death and how these fatal falls could have been prevented.

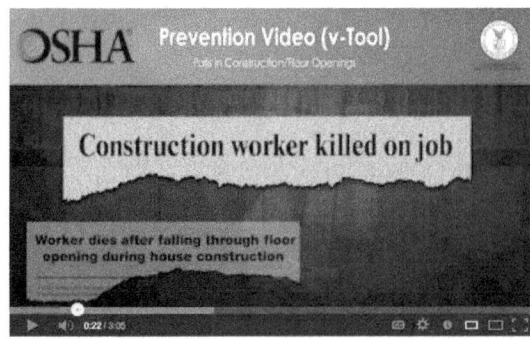

These training tools (v-Tools) support why using the right type of fall protection equipment will enable workers to go home the same way they came to work that day.

You can download the following videos, view the transcripts or view them on YouTube:

Falls in Construction

- Floor Openings
- Fixed Scaffolds
- Bridge Decking
- Reroofing
- Leading Edge Work

Fall Prevention Fact Sheet – English

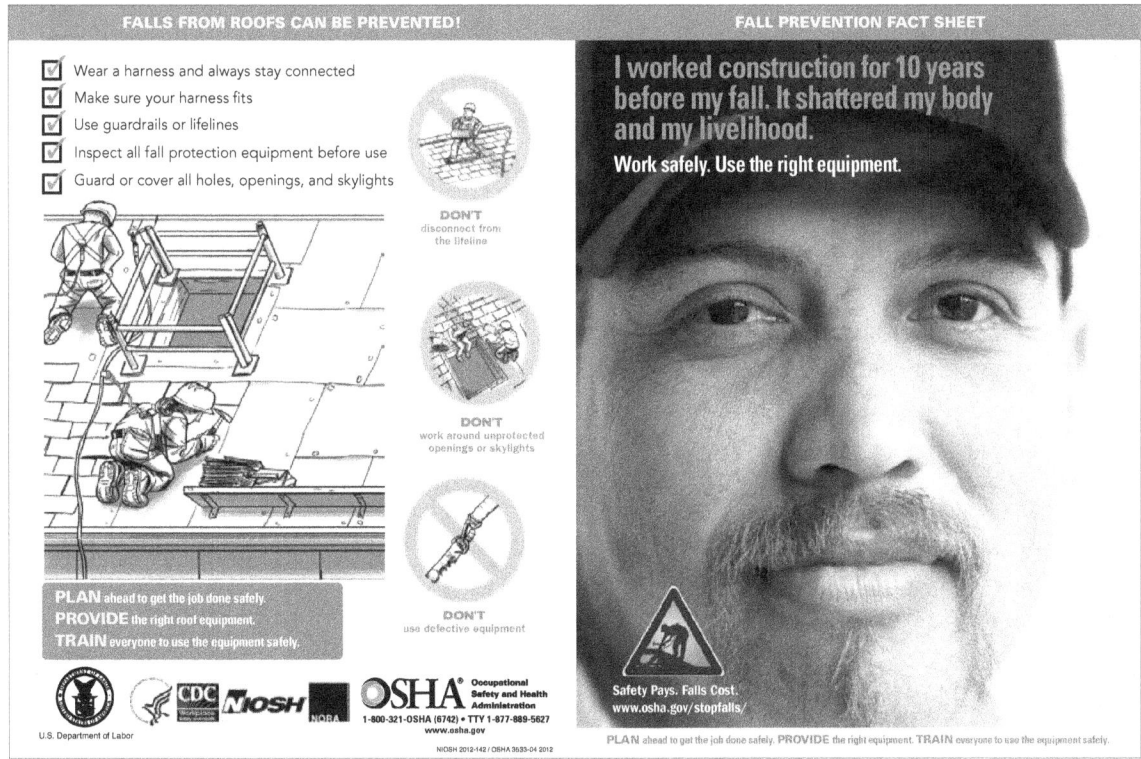

Una hoja informativa—Prevención contra caídas – Español

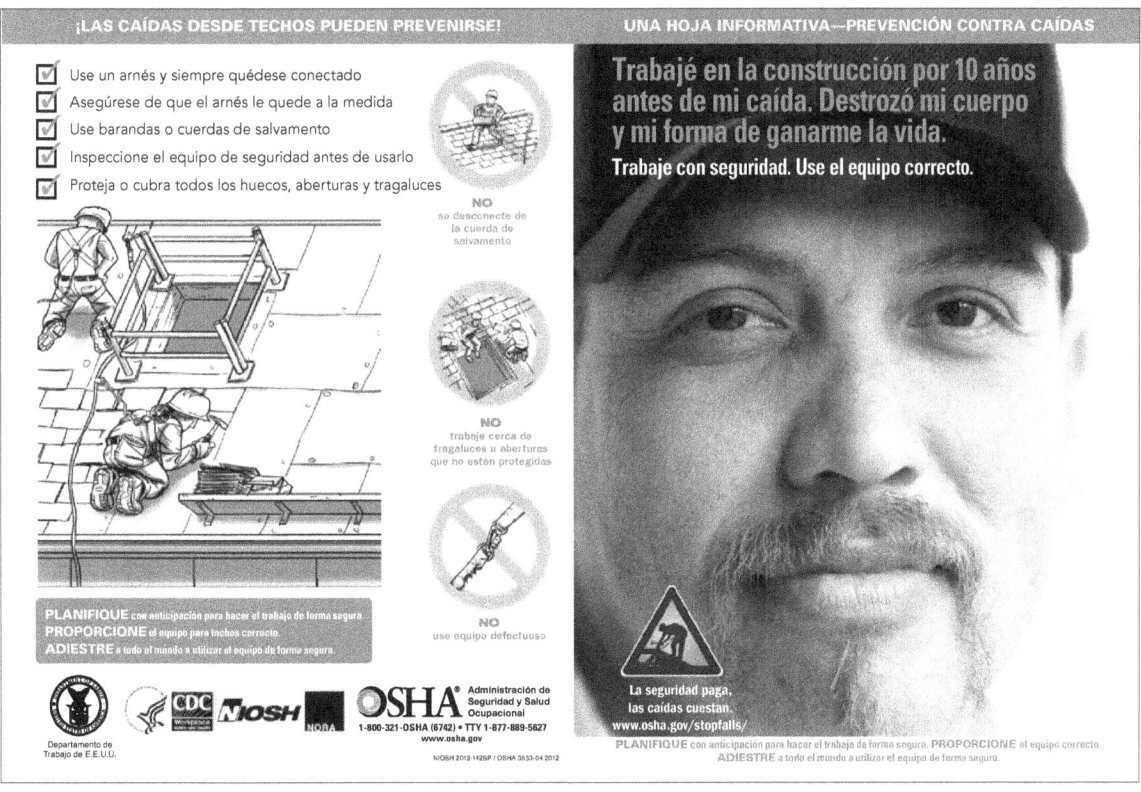

Fall Prevention Wallet Card – English

**PLAN.
PROVIDE.
TRAIN.**

Falls from ladders, scaffolds and roofs can be prevented!

www.osha.gov/stopfalls

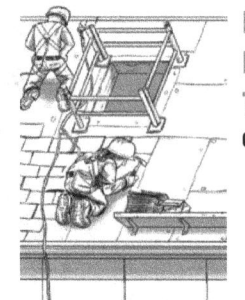

PLAN ahead to get the job done safely.
PROVIDE the right equipment.
TRAIN everyone to use the equipment safely.

OSHA 3557-06 2012

www.osha.gov/stopfalls 800-321-OSHA (6742) TTY 1-877-889-5627

Tarjeta sobre la prevención contra caídas – Español

**PLANIFIQUE
PROPORCIONE
ADIESTRE**

¡Las caídas desde escaleras, andamios y techos pueden ser prevenidas!

www.osha.gov/stopfalls

PLANIFIQUE con anticipación para hacer el trabajo de forma segura.
PROPORCIONE el equipo correcto.
ADIESTRE a todo el mundo a utilizar el equipo de forma segura.

OSHA 3564-05R 2013 - Spanish

www.osha.gov/stopfalls 800-321-OSHA (6742) TTY 1-877-889-5627

Cartão de prevenção contra quedas – Portuguese

**PLANEJE.
FORNEÇA.
TREINE.**

As quedas de escadas, andaimes e telhados podem ser prevenidas!

www.osha.gov/stopfalls

PLANEJE antes para fazer o trabalho com segurança.
FORNEÇA o equipamento correto.
TREINE todo mundo na utilização segura do equipamento.

OSHA 3664-05 2013 - Portuguese

www.osha.gov/stopfalls 800-321-OSHA (6742) TTY 1-877-889-5627

Fall Prevention Poster – English

Prevención de caídas—Cartel – Español

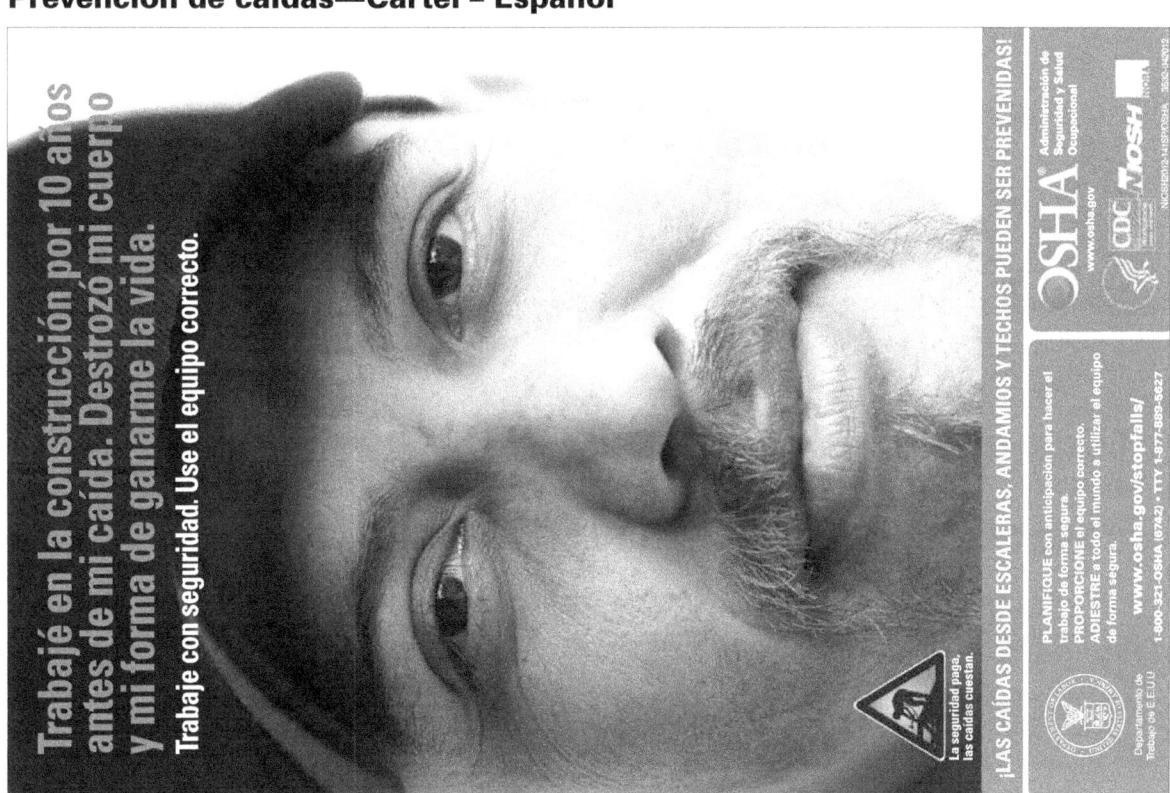

Falling Off Ladders Can Kill:
Use Them Safely

Las caídas desde escaleras pueden ser mortales:
Úselas de forma segura

www.osha.gov/stopfalls
www.osha.gov/stopfalls/spanish

OSHA 3625-03 2013

Falls from ladders, scaffolds and roofs can be prevented

Las caídas desde escaleras, andamios y techos pueden prevenirse

PLAN ahead to get the job done safely.

PROVIDE the right equipment.

TRAIN everyone to use the equipment safely.

For more information, visit www.osha.gov/stopfalls or www.osha.gov/stopfalls/spanish.

www.ingramcontent.com/pod-product-compliance
Lightning Source LLC
Chambersburg PA
CBHW081757170526
45167CB00009B/4057